Language Arts Pre-K-3

Readiness • Reading • Writing • Spelling • Phonics •

Over 300 Pre-K Readiness
Activities for Little Learners

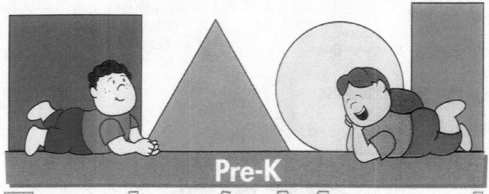

Pre-K

Teacher's Manual

for

Readiness Lane Activities

and

Alphabet Lane Activities

Authors

Sue Dickson,

Vida Daly,

Susan Nitz,

and

Jeanette Cason

Modern Curriculum Press, an imprint of Pearson Learning

299 Jefferson Road, P.O. Box 480, Parsippany, NJ 07054

1-800-321-3106 / www.pearsonlearning.com

ISBN: 1-56704-644-4

ILS gratefully acknowledges the following for their contributions:

Consultants
Jeanette Cason
Dianne Fix

Editor
Susan Nitz, Sr. Editor

Illustrators
Leigh Anderson
Nathan Heim
Paul Rosado
Gregory Dwayne Dyer

Production Support
Jane Allen

Music
Songs and Lyrics
Sue Dickson
Arranger and Producer
Stephen Peppos
Danny Hamilton

SSR&W Singers
Bobby Dickson
Christina Dickson
Kaleigh Dickson
Kara Dickson
Brittany Mayes

Sing Spell Read & Write

Teacher's Manual for *Readiness Lane* and *Alphabet Lane* Activities

Table of Contents

PRESCHOOL READINESS ACTIVITIES FOR LITTLE LEARNERS

OVERVIEW: Scope & Sequence

The theme of the **Preschool Readiness Activities for Little Learners** age 4 is a *Jolly Trolley* ride down *Readiness Lane* and *Alphabet Lane*. A colorful scope and sequence chart is on a large map of "Jolly Trolley Land". It shows Readiness Lane, Alphabet Lane, four **Musical Math Houses,** and all the skills activities to be introduced. The hands-on, multisensory learning activities were designed keeping in mind the capabilities and limitations of four-year-old children: their coordination, the length of their attention span, the appeal and familiarity of the topics, and the need for simplicity. The Preschool teacher will move the *Jolly Trolley* icon forward along the lanes of readiness where the children participate in multisensory, hands-on developmental readiness activities to help them learn colors, shapes, and all other concepts necessary to get ready to learn to read.

Placemat Side 1

Placemat Side 2

The Readiness Activities for Little Learners also includes the following:

- A to Z Phonics Song Wall Cards**
- Sing Along Songs on Cassette** and CD
- A to Z Wall Cards**
- Alph-O Cards
- Award Stickers*
- Math Counting Sticks
- Daily Individual Little Learner "Do and Take Home" Activity Materials*
- Clock Manipulative with moving hour hand
- Shoe Manipulative with lace to tie
- Alph-O Puzzles
- Sing Along & Point Placemat (2 sides/2 songs)
- Sing along and point strip with Alphabet and Number Line (2 sides/2 songs)

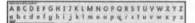

Sing Along and Point Strip - ABCs

Sing Along and Point Strip - Math

*Consumable
** In classroom program only

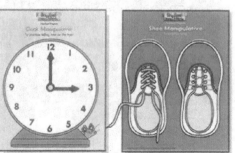

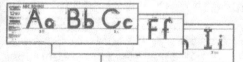

PRESCHOOL READINESS ACTIVITIES FOR LITTLE LEARNERS

182 *Readiness Lane* Activities for Preschool Learners (PreK-1)

Each of the concepts and related activities for **Readiness Lane** is presented to assist preschool children in learning:

- Colors
- Shapes
- Visual Discrimination
- Matching
- Opposites
- Classification
- Sequence
- Seasons

107 *Alphabet Lane* Activities for Preschool Learners (PreK-2)

Alphabet Lane Activities are designed to follow **Readiness Lane Activities**, and will present young learners with pre-reading and math readiness activities that assist preschool children in:

- Letter recognition
- Phonemic awareness
- Coloring
- Large-object tracing
- Listening with discernment
- Auditory discrimination
- Oral vocabulary development
- Counting to ten (1-10)
- Counting backwards (10-1)
- Learning the concept of zero (0)

PRESCHOOL READINESS ACTIVITIES FOR LITLE LEARNERS

Parental Components

School and Home Hands-On Activities

At school, preschool children learn readiness skills through hands-on group and individual activities. They have activities to do, take home, and show parents what they are learning at school.

Award Stickers

Included in the program is an AWARDS component with sheets of "stick-on prize buttons." These are the children's "badges of accomplishment" as they finish a readiness section. For example, after the section on Colors is completed, each child is awarded the "button" that says, "I learned about colors." It will be a visible memento to show their family and friends that they have accomplished something special when they proudly wear it home.

There are other "prize buttons" to be awarded when the children are ready: "I know my name in print," meaning that they recognize their name in manuscript, etc.

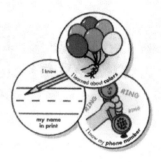

The emphasis with "prize button" awards is the very positive one of rewarding the children for completing the activities along with the class, rather than for mastering knowledge of all the shapes, understanding all the concepts, or being able to arrange every sequence story in order. They completed their first readiness collection, and hopefully, it was a happy and rewarding experience.

Preschool Teacher's Manual

The **Preschool Teacher's Manual** is the key resource for each multisensory, preschool activity designed to help children gain readiness skills through a special sequence of hands-on learning. For example, 46 different activities are provided in the manual to help the young child understand the concept of *Opposites*. Forty-four activities, including five recorded *sing along and march* songs, are provided to lead children to recognize *Shapes*. Suggestions for correlated arts and crafts, bulletin boards, related poems, songs, and games, as well as lists of **Recommended Read Aloud** library books are included in the manual. Reading the stories to children will help to expand their knowledge of the concepts explored.

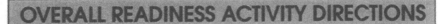

OVERALL READINESS ACTIVITY DIRECTIONS

- **There are over 300 activities** in the **Readiness Activities for Little Learners. They are designed to be led by a teacher or assistant.** They may be used with a total group, small group, or individual children.

- Teacher directions are included in this manual for each activity.

- In helping the children understand new concepts, there will be many opportunities for discussions and exchanges of ideas. These will broaden the children's knowledge and help to expand their vocabulary.

- When there are several directions to be presented for an activity, be sure to give just one at a time, allowing the children the opportunity to follow the first direction before the next is presented. (Later, children will learn to follow a sequence of two, then three directions.)

- Some children will want to color when the activities do not particularly specify coloring. Let them. They may enjoy doing this independently after a concept is explored and the activity completed with the teacher and group.

- **All of the preschool activities are designed so that young learners experience success right from the start.** As they are guided through the daily activities, teachers can relax knowing the children are being led step-by-step to readiness for reading. At the conclusion of the Shapes Activities, there may be some children who are not able to tell a square from a rectangle. There is no need to press them. They have been exposed to it and when it is presented again, it will seem like an old friend, and they will be mature enough to understand better.

- The songs are recorded on cassette and CD. SHEET MUSIC for the A to Z Phonics Song and lyrics for all other songs are included beginning on p. 65.

NOTES

Readiness Lane
Preschool Readiness Activities

36 HANDS-ON ACTIVITIES TO LEARN COLORS

Trolley Stop Activities 1A to 11B
Objective

To provide hands-on, motivational group and individual experiences and activities to guide preschool children to learn to:
- recognize and name colors
- understand how some items are always the same color
- classify items by color

Recommended Read Aloud Literature

*The Little **Red** Hen* -Treasury of Virtues

*Little **Red** Riding Hood* -Treasury of Virtues

*The Lion and the Little **Red** Bird* by Elisa Kleven

*A **Color** of His Own* by Leo Lionni

***Brown** Bear, **Brown** Bear, What Do You See?* By Bill Martin, Jr.

*A **Rainbow** of My Own* by Don Freeman

*One fish, two fish, **red** fish, **blue** fish* by Dr. Seuss

*I Love **Colors*** by Stan & Jan Berenstain

*The Little Mouse, the **Red** Ripe Strawberry, and the Big Hungry Bear* by Don and Audry Wood

***Green** Eggs and Ham* by Dr. Seuss

Caps for Sale by Esphyr Slobodkina

***White** Rabbit's Color Book* by Alan Baker

1. Introducing each Color
- Hold up a balloon, a large piece of paper, and several other objects of the color being taught.
- Ask the children how many know the name of the color for these objects. Have them say the name.
- Have the children wearing the color stand up.
- Next, ask the children to find things in the room that are that color.
- Talk about things outside the room or daycare center that are that color. (Examples for red: red fire engine, red traffic light, red Santa Claus suit, etc.)

HANDS-ON ACTIVITIES TO LEARN COLORS Continued

COLORS SONG

Introduce "Colors Song" on Cassette or CD. Lyrics in Music section, TM p. 66. Invite the group to sit up close to the Jolly Trolley Chart. Sing along and point to the colors and objects representing that color on the Chart, following the song. Choose a leader to point along with the chart as the rest of the group sings.

- Distribute Jolly Trolley Chart Placemats and have children point along to colors and objects and sing "Colors Song".
- Have children color the three items for Color Recognition, Trolley Stop Activities 1A to 11A as each color is introduced.
- Color Classification, Trolley Stop Activities 1B to 11B will have some items that are not the color the children are learning today. Discuss the color of each item. Circle the items that are the "color of the day." Cross out the items that are not the "color of the day."
- Next, have the children color the circled pictures.
- Move the trolley to the next stop on the Jolly Trolley Chart as each color is introduced.

Color Recognition
Trolley Stop Activity 1A

2. Clown Bulletin Board

Materials needed:
Colored construction paper
Yarn
Stapler

- On a bulletin board, pin up a big clown made from construction paper, using yarn for his hair and the tassel on his hat.
- Cut a circle of each color, and staple these above the clown's head as balloons.
- Use yarn for string leading from the clown's hands to each balloon.
- Play a game where one child says, "Please buy me a red balloon." Then he/she picks a child who points out the red balloon with a pointer.
- Later this game may be played with the child asking for two or even three colors.

Color Classification
Trolley Stop Activity 1B

Readiness Lane
Preschool Readiness Activities

HANDS-ON ACTIVITIES TO LEARN COLORS Continued

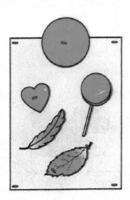

3. Color Wall Charts

Materials needed:
Oaktag for chart
Old magazines to cut up
Assorted craft items: feathers, buttons,
yarn, fabric scraps, colored paper scraps
Glue

Place a large circle of a particular color at the top of a chart and have the children bring items of that color to be glued on it – cloth, paper, yarn, feathers, plastic, etc. Pictures of items of that color may be glued on it, too.

4. Animal Color Books

Materials needed:
Old animal books or nature magazines to cut up
Scissors
Glue
Paper

Collect pictures of animals or insects that are green or live in green surroundings (or in brown surroundings), animals that have orange on them, black and white animals, etc. Make a book. Group animals of the same color on the same page.

5. Food Train Bulletin Board

Materials needed:
Colored construction paper
Old magazines to cut up
Stapler

- Make a train with cars of different colors for the bulletin board.
- Print a color word on each car of the train.
- Have children cut pictures of fruits and vegetables from old magazines.
- Staple pictures on the proper train cars.

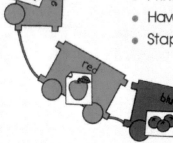

Readiness Lane
Preschool Readiness Activities

6. Color Magic: Mm, Good!

Materials needed:
Prepared vanilla frosting
Three bowls
Food coloring (red, blue, yellow)
Spoons
Clear plastic cups
Crackers

- Fill three bowls with vanilla frosting.
- Have children stir red food coloring into one bowl, yellow into the second, and blue into the third.
- Give a clear plastic cup and spoon to each child.
- Have children experiment with mixing the colored frosting.
- Eventually a child will come up with green, orange, or purple. Recall with the student which two colors were mixed to result in that particular color.
- Have children tell others how that color was made.
- When children are finished spread the colored frosting on crackers for a snack.
- While they eat, read the book *Green Eggs and Ham* by Dr. Seuss.

7. Favorite Color Chart

Materials needed:
Large paper for chart
Glue
Colored construction paper
Scissors

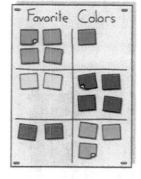

- Make a chart for the color preferences of the children. See illustration.
- Cut several small squares of each color.
- Have children come up and take a square of their favorite color.
- Have students paste the squares under the favorite color.

Readiness Lane
Preschool Readiness Activities

8. Color Stories

Materials needed:
Paper for booklets
Crayons

Read this poem aloud to children:
> Red says "stop" on the traffic light.
> Red is the sun when it sets big and bright.
> Red is the fire engine whizzing down the street.
> Red is an apple that I love to eat.
> Red is a color in our country's flag.
> Red are my cheeks when I run and play tag!

- Have students illustrate their favorite lines from the poem.
- Compose poems for other colors and follow same procedure.

9. Line-Up Time Game

When you dismiss the children, say, "All those wearing blue may get their coats," "All those wearing yellow may line up," etc.

10. Hand Print Mural

Materials needed:
Tempera paints and brushes
Two or three yards bulletin board paper

- Attach paper to bulletin board.
- Place a jar of each color of paint on a table (protected with newspaper or plastic).
- Have the girls and boys pick partners and go up to a table a few couples at a time.
- One child chooses a favorite color and the partner paints the palm of the child's hand.
- Next, the child puts his or her handprint up on the bulletin board.
- Let everyone watch as this patterns into a fascinating mural!

HANDS-ON ACTIVITIES TO LEARN COLORS Continued

11. Role Play

Materials needed:
Paper plates
Brushes and Paint (several colors)
Book - *Caps for Sale* by Esphyr Slobodkina

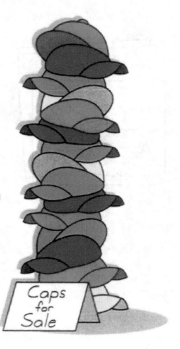

- Have children paint the paper plates different colors.

- Read *Caps for Sale*.

- Choose one person to be the peddler and some others to be monkeys. The monkeys form a line and the peddler walks down the street carrying a stack of colored paper plates (the caps) which the children have previously painted.

- The peddler walks around calling, "Caps for sale! Caps for sale!" Nobody buys any, so the peddler sits by the side of the road with the "caps" and takes a nap.

- While the peddler sleeps, the monkeys tiptoe up and steal the caps. The peddler wakes up and tells the monkeys to return the caps, but they just chatter. The peddler shakes a finger at them; they do the same back. The peddler stamps his or her feet, jumps up and down, etc., following every action in the story. Each time the monkeys mimic the peddler.

- Finally, the peddler gets very angry and slams down his or her cap, and the monkeys do the same. Then the peddler picks up all the caps, saying each color while doing so.

- When all the caps are in a pile, the peddler hands them to another child who will be the peddler, and each monkey chooses another child to take a place in the line.

12. Snack Suggestions:

red - apple
yellow - banana
blue - blueberry muffins
brown - brownies or chocolate milk
green or purple -grapes
orange - orange slices
black - licorice
pink - strawberry ice cream
white - vanilla ice cream

HANDS-ON ACTIVITIES TO LEARN COLORS Continued

13. Color Riddles:

I rhyme with red.
You sleep on me.
What am I? (bed)

I rhyme with yellow.
I come in different colors.
I wiggle and squiggle.
You eat me.
What am I? (jello)

I rhyme with blue.
You wear me on your foot.
What am I? (shoe)

I rhyme with brown.
When I am sad,
I may have this on my face.
What am I? (frown)

I rhyme with green.
I am green.
You eat me.
What am I? (bean)

I come from a round fruit.
I am orange.
You drink me for breakfast.
What am I? (orange juice)

I am purple.
I can also be green.
I am round and come in clusters.
You eat me.
What am I? (grapes)

I rhyme with black.
I am part of your body.
I am not in the front, but in the
(back).

I rhyme with pink.
You can do this with your eyes.
What am I? (wink)

I rhyme with gray.
I like to do this with a friend.
We do this on the playground.
What am I? (play)

I rhyme with white.
When we go to bed,
I am there.
What am I? (night)

14. Color Pattern Manipulative

Materials needed:
White paper   Construction paper - 2 colors   Glue

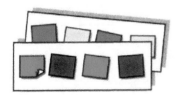

- Give each child a 6" x 18" strip of white paper and four 2"
  squares of colored paper; two each of two different colors.
- Have children paste the pictures in a pattern. Example: red,
  blue, red, blue.
- Vary this activity using different color combinations.

NOTES

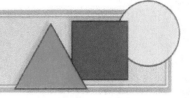

44 HANDS-ON ACTIVITIES TO LEARN SHAPES

Trolley Stop Activities 12A to 15N

Objective

To provide hands-on, motivational group and individual experiences and activities to guide preschool children to learn to:

- recognize the four basic shapes: circle, square, triangle, rectangle
- name the four basic shapes
- classify items by shape

Recommended Read Aloud Literature

Shapes, Shapes, Shapes by Tana Hoban

*The **Shape** of Me and Other Stuff* by Dr. Seuss

*Brown Rabbit's **Shape** Book* by Alan Baker

The Wheels on the Bus by Maryann Kovalski

The four basic shapes (circle, square, triangle, rectangle) are presented in this section. There are several activities for each shape. **These activities will teach shape recognition, classification, following directions, visual discrimination, and matching. Spend approximately one week studying each shape until all are known.** As each new shape is presented, the key word should be repeated in every sentence of instruction. Follow the activities in order, as there is a sequence to the teaching.

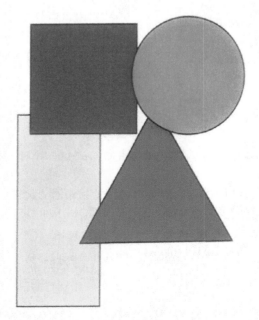

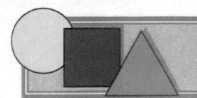

Readiness Lane
Preschool Readiness Activities

HANDS-ON ACTIVITIES TO LEARN SHAPES Continued

1. Introducing the Shapes

- Hold up a three dimensional item of that shape and the shape cut from construction paper (Example: a round ball and a circle cut from construction paper).
- Ask the children how many know the name of the shape and let them say the name.
- Next, ask them to find things in the classroom that are that shape.
- Discuss things outside the room or daycare center that are that shape. (Example: coins, plates, oranges, apples, wheels, etc.)
- Have children color the shape for Shape Recognition, Trolley Stop Activity 12A.
- Next, have children complete the Shape Trace Over for Trolley Stop Activity 12B to make a shape.
- Shape Classification, Trolley Stop Activity 12C will contain some shapes that are not the "shape of the day." Follow the directions for each shape.
- Move the trolley to the next stop on the Jolly Trolley Chart.
- Continue the same procedure for Trolley Stop Activities 13A to 15C.
- Trolley Stop Activities 15D-15N provide a review of the four shapes including Shape Recognition, Visual Discrimination, and Following Directions.

2. Shapes and Color Building

Materials needed:
Oaktag
Crayons
Glue
Construction paper

- Give each child a small oaktag circle.
- Have children paste their circles in the center of a piece of construction paper.
- Next, have children draw as many concentric circles around the oaktag circle until it is as large as the paper will permit.
- Have children name the colors of each circle.
- This same activity should be used with the square, triangle, and rectangle.

Trolley Stop Activity 12A

Trolley Stop Activity 12B

Trolley Stop Activity 12C

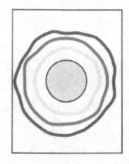

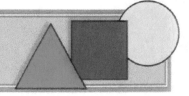

HANDS-ON ACTIVITIES TO LEARN SHAPES Continued

3. Clay Shapes

Materials needed:
Clay

Have children roll clay into a long "snake" and make various shapes.

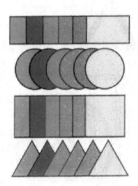

4. Flannel Board Shapes

Materials needed:
Flannel board
Colored flannel shapes

- Teacher will cut out 6 flannel circles, squares, triangles, and rectangles of assorted colors.
- Stick assorted shapes on a flannel board.
- Have children remove all the circles, all the squares, etc.

5. Shape Walk

Take a "shape" walk and have children discover how many shapes they can find in buildings, trees, flowers, vehicles, etc.

Triangle

Circle

Rectangle

6. Shape Bulletin Board

Materials needed:
Old magazines to cut up
Scissors

- Divide the children into committees.
- Each member of the "circle" committee is responsible for finding at least one example of that shape in a magazine. Other shape committees will do the same.
- Exhibit pictures on a bulletin board under the correct heading.

Sing Spell
Read & Write.

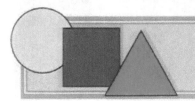

Readiness Lane
Preschool Readiness Activities

HANDS-ON ACTIVITIES TO LEARN SHAPES Continued

7. The Shapes Song and March

Materials needed:
Masking tape
Cassette or CD: "Circle Song", "Rectangle Song", "Square Song", "Triangle Song", "Shape Review Song"
Lyrics in Music section, TM pp. 67-68

- Make a large "shape of the day" on the floor with masking tape (approx. 8 feet on each side).
- Discuss the shape with children (a square has four corners and four sides, etc.)
- Invite a few children at a time to march on the "shape of the day" while the group sings the "Square Song, etc.".

- Sing the song for the shape often during the week it is presented.
- When all the shapes have been introduced, the children are ready to review the shapes singing the "Shape Review Song".
- To sing the "Shape Review Song", form the shapes on the floor with masking tape as illustrated.
- Suggestion: When singing and marching, provide instruments that represent the different shapes for the children to play: tambourine or cymbals for circle, triangle for triangle, sandpaper blocks for rectangle.

8. Pegboard Shapes

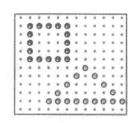

Materials needed:
Pegboards and pegs

Use pegboards and make a square with blue pegs, then a triangle with red pegs, etc.

9. Sandpaper Collage

Materials needed:
Sandpaper
Oaktag
Glue
Scissors

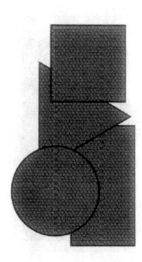

- Cut a circle, square, triangle, and rectangle out of sandpaper.
- Glue each shape on oaktag.
- Have children close their eyes, feel the shape, and tell what shape it is.

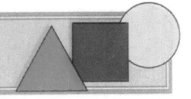

HANDS-ON ACTIVITIES TO LEARN SHAPES Continued

- Vary this activity by cutting shapes out of styrofoam or foam rubber. Place all of the shapes in a bag. Have children close their eyes, feel a shape in the bag, and tell which shape they chose (without looking).

10. Shape Tree

Materials needed:
Small tree branch
Pebbles or sand
Spray paint
Colored shapes

- Spray paint a bare branch with many twigs.
- Place branch in can.
- Fill can with pebbles or sand.
- Hang colored shapes on tree.

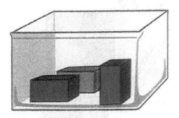

11. Sorting Shapes

Materials needed:
Three plastic containers - one round, one square, and one rectangular
Blocks - square, round, and rectangular

Have the children place the round blocks in the round container, square blocks in square container, and rectangular blocks in rectangular container.

12. Shape Hopscotch

Materials needed:
Colored masking tape

- Make a "shape" hopscotch for your floor with masking tape. "Draw" a circle, square, etc.
- Choose someone to give directions. "Skip to the blue triangle." "Hop to the green triangle," etc.

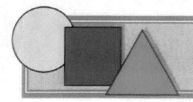

Readiness Lane
Preschool Readiness Activities

HANDS-ON ACTIVITIES TO LEARN SHAPES Continued

13. Shape Puzzles

Materials needed:
Styrofoam meat trays
knife (for adult use only)

- On each tray, draw a circle, square, triangle, or rectangle.
- Teacher will cut out the shapes with a knife.
- Spread out puzzles.
- Have children take turns finding the shape to match each tray.

14. Jello Shapes

Materials needed:
Four different flavors of Jello gelatin
Shallow pans
Knife
Spatula

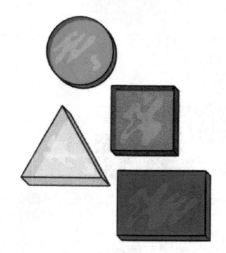

- Prepare gelatin according to box directions.
- Pour each flavor into a separate shallow pan.
- Allow gelatin to chill until firm.
- Cut circles, squares, triangles, and rectangles. Remove shapes from pans with spatula.
- Serve to children and ask them to identify shapes.

15. Caterpillar Picture

Materials needed:
Green construction paper
Glue
9 x 12 paper

- Cut enough circles for each child to have six green circles of different sizes.
- Have children glue the circles on a 9 x 12 sheet of paper to make a caterpillar.
- Teacher should make the first one as a model for the children.
- Encourage the children to use the largest circle for the face.

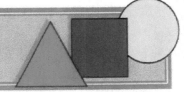

HANDS-ON ACTIVITIES TO LEARN SHAPES Continued

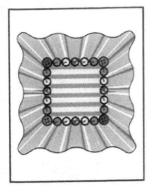

16. Shape Decorations

Materials needed:
White construction paper
Variety of material for decorating (foil, fabric or paper scraps, buttons, sequins, tissue paper, etc,)

- Give each child a sheet of paper with a large shape drawn on it.
- Have children decorate their shapes with materials provided.

17. Popcorn Balls

Materials needed:
$^1/_4$ lb. butter
12 $^1/_2$ oz. pkg. miniature marshmallows
salt
5 cups popped corn
1 pkg. small gumdrops

Melt the marshmallows in heated butter. Let cool and stir in the popped corn and gumdrops. Place a few drops of cooking oil on each child's hand. Give each child a heaping tablespoon of the mixture. Roll or press into different shapes (circle, square, triangle, rectangle).

18. Body Shapes

Have children lie down on the floor to make different shapes (circle, square, triangle, rectangle).

19. Keep the Ball in the Circle Game

Materials needed:
8 $^1/_2$" playground ball

Have children sit in a circle. The children must keep the ball from leaving the circle without using their hands. They must stop the ball with their feet and kick it to another person. Have the children lean back on their hands to gain foot power. This is an excellent gross motor activity.

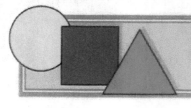

NOTES

25 HANDS-ON ACTIVITIES TO LEARN VISUAL DISCRIMINATION & MATCHING

Trolley Stop Activities 16A-T

Objective

To provide hands-on, motivational group and individual experiences and activities to guide preschool children to learn to recognize:

- alike and different
- size
- direction
- sequence
- objects that match

Recommended Read Aloud Literature

*You and Me, **Little** Bear* by Martin Waddell

*The **Big** Sneeze* by Ruth Brown

The Grouchy Ladybug by Eric Carle

The activities on the following two pages provide an important step in helping children to see likenesses and differences, which will lead them to develop their discriminating powers in learning to see the differences between alphabet letters.

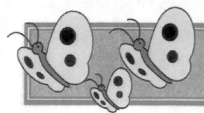

HANDS-ON ACTIVITIES TO LEARN VISUAL DISCRIMINATION & MATCHING Continued

1. Size

- Hold up three pencils, two of the same size and one of them different.
- Talk about the pencils: "How can you tell the two that are alike?"
- Ask the children which pencil is different and why.
- Use other examples: 3 different size sheets of construction paper, 3 different size books, 3 different size toys, etc.
- Have children name the pictures on Trolley Stop Activity 16A and tell how one picture is different. Example: Two grasshoppers are big and one grasshopper is small.
- Talk about other words that mean the same as "big" i.e. large, huge, gigantic, etc.
- Talk about other words that mean the same as "small" i.e. tiny, little, etc.
- Have students circle the picture that is different.
- Next, have students color the pictures.
- Follow the directions on Trolley Stop Activities 16B to 16C and continue.

Trolley Stop Activity 16A

2. Direction

- Have 3 children form a line, with one facing a different direction.
- Ask the children which one is facing a different direction and why they know it's different.
- Use other examples: toy trucks or cars, bears, dolls, etc.
- Have children name the pictures on Trolley Stop Activity 16D and place their fingers on the two animals facing the same direction.
- Next, have students draw a line under the two animals facing the same direction and color.
- Follow the directions on Trolley Stop Activities 16E to 16G and continue.

Trolley Stop Activity 16D

3. Alike and Different

- Hold up three pencils, two unsharpened and one sharpened.
- Ask the children which one is different and why.

HANDS-ON ACTIVITIES TO LEARN VISUAL DISCRIMINATION & MATCHING Continued

Trolley Stop Activity 16H

- Have children name the pictures on Trolley Stop Activities 16H and tell how one picture is different. Examples: One lion has no tail and one lamb is missing a leg.
- Have students circle the items that are different and then color the pictures.
- Follow the directions on Trolley Stop Activities 16I to 16K and continue in the same manner.

4. Sequence

- Have 3 children stand in a line.
- Introduce and discuss "first, middle, and last" using the children as examples. "Who is in the middle?", "Who comes last?", "Who is first?"
- Choose additional items from the classroom for more practice. Be sure to use concrete objects (chairs, books on a bookshelf, a row of toy trucks, blocks, pictures on the chalkboard, flannel board, etc.) For example, let a child put a chair in the middle of the room, talk about waking up in the middle of the night, etc.
- Have the children identify the items on Trolley Stop Activity 16L, then color the chair that comes first and circle the doll that is in the middle.
- Follow the directions on Trolley Stop Activities 16M to 16N and continue.

Trolley Stop Activity 16L

5. Matching

This section carries over the idea of recognizing likenesses and differences. Note that each activity is a little more difficult than the one before.

- Have the children identify the items on Matching Fun Activity, Trolley Stop 16O.
- Direct them to draw a line from the object on one side to its matching object on the other side and then color the pictures.
- Follow the procedure above for Trolley Stop Activities 16P to 16T.
- Move the trolley to the next stop on the Jolly Trolley Chart.

Trolley Stop Activity 16O

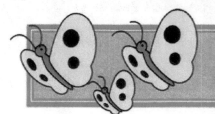

Readiness Lane
Preschool Readiness Activities

NOTES

_____
_____
_____
_____
_____
_____
_____
_____
_____
_____
_____
_____
_____
_____
_____
_____
_____
_____
_____
_____
_____
_____
_____
_____
_____
_____
_____

28

46 HANDS-ON ACTIVITIES TO LEARN OPPOSITES

Trolley Stop Activities 17A-X

Objective

To provide hands-on, motivational group and individual experiences and activities to guide preschool children to learn to identify opposites:

- big and little
- up and down
- over and under
- behind and In front of
- on and off
- etc.

Recommended Read Aloud Literature

The Little House by Virginia Burton

The Little Red Lighthouse and the Great Grey Bridge by Hildegarde Swift and Lynd Ward

The Biggest Bear by Lynd Ward

Little Toot by Hardie Gramatky

Ten Apples Up On Top! by Theo. LeSieg

Inside Outside Upside Down by Stan & Jan Berenstain

Old Hat New Hat by Stan & Jan Berenstain

Great Day for UP by Dr. Seuss

Above My Head, Beneath My Feet by K.D. Plum

The following concepts on pages 30-38 are presented in an effort to help the children develop the ability to identify opposites, perceive relationships, and promote visual discrimination.

HANDS-ON ACTIVITIES TO LEARN OPPOSITES Continued

1. BIG and LITTLE

- Suggest that the children think of big animals and little animals. Try to elicit as many examples from them as possible.
- Have someone find a big book and a little book, a big toy and a little toy, etc.
- Have one child take ten big steps and another child take ten little steps and compare the distance they covered.
- Go outdoors and find a big tree and a little tree, a big house and a small house, a big flower and a small flower, etc.
- Children will name the items for Big and Little, Trolley Stop Activity 17A and tell which animal is big (elephant) and which is little (frog). Next, color the items.
- Follow the directions for Trolley Stop Activities 17B to 17D and continue in the same manner.

Trolley Stop Activity 17A

2. Big and Little Chart Activity

Materials needed:
Chart paper or poster board
Pictures of "big" items and "small" items
Glue

- Label one chart the "Big" chart and paste a picture of an elephant at the top.
- Label the second chart the "Little" chart and paste a picture of a frog at the top.
- Discuss with the children which pictures belong on the "Big" chart and which pictures belong on the "Little" chart. Separate the pictures into two piles.
- Have the children paste the pictures on the appropriate chart.

3. Synonyms for Big

Talk about other words that mean the same as "big" i.e. large, giant, huge, great. (You may choose to write these words on the "Big" chart described above, or make a new chart made up of words only.) The children won't be able to read the words, but they will love giving you lots of synonyms and watching you write them all down.

LARGE
GIANT
HUGE

HANDS-ON ACTIVITIES TO LEARN OPPOSITES Continued

Small
Teenie
Tiny

4. Synonyms for Small
Talk about other words that mean the same as "little" i.e. small, teeny, tiny, wee, etc. (You may choose to write these words on the "Little" chart described above, or make a separate word chart.)

5. UP and DOWN
- Choose objects in the room and help the children decide if they are "up" or "down."
- Have children think of some things that go up and down, i.e. a window, a bouncing ball, a seesaw, an elevator, a yo-yo, a light switch, the sun, etc.
- Demonstrate as many examples as possible. Actually bounce a ball with the children and watch it go up and down, have two children make-believe they are on a seesaw and watch them move up and down, etc.
- The children will draw an X on the bird that is up in the tree for Trolley Stop Activity 17E. Next, the children will color the bird that is down on the ground.

Trolley Stop Activity 17E

6. OVER and UNDER
- Pick a child to crawl over a table, and another one to crawl under it.
- Take turns bouncing a ball over a chair and then rolling it under a chair.
- Line up several children and let them pass a toy under their legs, then back over their heads.
- Take a jump rope out on the playground. Let a child hold it at each end, about a foot and a half off the ground. Have some children step over the rope, and others crawl under the rope.
- Read the Nursery Rhyme "Hey Diddle Diddle". Have the children pretend they are the cow jumping over the moon.
- Read the Nursery Rhyme "Jack Be Nimble". Have the children pretend they are Jack jumping over the candlestick.
- The children will identify and color the clown jumping over the other clown for Trolley Stop Activity 17F. Next, the children will place an X on the balloon under the chair.

Trolley Stop Activity 17F

Readiness Lane
Preschool Readiness Activities

HANDS-ON ACTIVITIES TO LEARN OPPOSITES Continued

7. BEHIND and IN FRONT OF

- Have the children line up and pick the child in front of John, then the one behind him, etc.

- Take turns with someone standing in front of a chair, then behind a chair. Choose a variety of objects in the room you would like the children to practice with.

- Cut pictures out of catalogs of people, houses, cars, trees, animals, flowers, etc. Have the children paste the pictures to show flowers in front of a house, a car in front of a house, a car in front of a garage, a dog behind a fence, people behind a wall, a tree in front of a house, etc.

- Play music for the children to march to. The children will clap four times in front of their tummies, then clap four times behind their backs.

- The children will identify and color the child in front of the TV for Trolley Stop Activity 17G. Next, the children should identify and circle the child behind the TV.

Trolley Stop Activity 17G

8. IN FRONT OF and IN BACK OF

- Form a line with several children. Practice "in front of" and "in back of" using the children in line as examples.

- Using a toy train as an example, demonstrate that the engine is located in front of the train, and the caboose is located in back of the train.

- Draw a house on the board. Choose someone to draw a street in front of the house, and another to draw a garden in back of the house. You may continue this activity using other objects, i.e. tree, pond, car, etc.

- For Trolley Stop Activity 17H, the children will draw an X on the teddy bear in front of the doll. Next, instruct the children to draw a car in back of the bus.

Trolley Stop Activity 17H

9. ON and OFF

- Invite a child to place a blanket on a doll bed, then take it off.

- Ask how many children help put things on the table for supper, then help clear them off again. Encourage them to help their parents with this task daily.

- Pick a child to turn on the lights and another to turn them off, to turn on the water and turn it off again, write on the chalkboard and wipe it off again, etc.

HANDS-ON ACTIVITIES TO LEARN OPPOSITES Continued

Trolley Stop Activity 17I and 17J

- On the playground, have the children pretend they are getting on a bus, then off a bus, getting on an airplane, then getting off an airplane, etc.
- Help the children think of other things they (or their family members) turn on and off: computer, TV, camera, microwave, dishwasher, coffeemaker, oven, alarm clock, etc.
- Have the children identify the picture (scarecrow) and draw a hat on it for Trolley Stop Activity 17I. Next, the children will draw an X on the glove that is off the scarecrow.
- Follow the directions to complete Trolley Stop Activity 17J.

10. IN and OUT

- Choose a child to go out of a circle, then in it; out of the room and back in it, etc.
- On the playground, take turns doing the following: shovel sand in a bucket and then dump it out, take a ball outside and bring it inside again, etc.
- Have a child put a book in a desk and another child take it out; a toy in a box and out; a pencil in a drawer and out, etc.

LOOBY LOO SONG

Play "Looby Loo" on cassette or CD, emphasizing <u>in</u> and <u>out</u>. "Looby Loo" lyrics in Music section, TM p. 69.

- The children must color the lion in the cage for Trolley Stop Activity 17K.
- Follow the directions to complete Trolley Stop Activity 17L.

Trolley Stop Activity 17K and 17L

11. OPEN and CLOSE

- As a rule, children are very familiar with this concept. Have the children tell which windows are open and which are closed; take a book from the bookshelf and open it, then close it.
- Let the children open jars of different sizes, then close them; open the box, then close the box; open the drawer, close the drawer, etc.
- Have the children open their mouths, then close them; close their eyes, then open them; open their hands, then shut them, etc.
- For Trolley Stop Activity 17M, the children will draw a picture on the book that is closed. Next, the children will draw a ball in the toy chest that is open.

Trolley Stop Activity 17M

HANDS-ON ACTIVITIES TO LEARN OPPOSITES Continued

12. LONG and SHORT

- Note how many girls have long hair and how many have short hair; how many children are wearing long sleeves and how many are wearing short sleeves, etc. Point out who is wearing long pants, who is wearing shorts, etc.

- Help the children think of animals with long necks (giraffe, zebra, horse, ostrich, deer, etc.)

- For Trolley Stop Activity 17N, the children will draw a kite on the string that is long. Next, the children will draw a balloon on the string that is short.

- Ask how many children have ever flown a kite. Talk about long and short kite strings/tails. Talk about the last time they received or saw balloons (birthday party, circus, supermarket) Did they have long or short strings?

- Talk about long and short trips, long and short storybooks, etc.

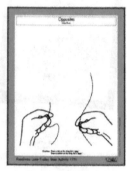

Trolley Stop Activity 17N

13. HIGH and LOW

- Help the children think of things that fly high in the sky: airplanes, hot air balloons, helicopters, etc.

- Help the children think of things that ride low to the ground: trains, cars, motorcycles, trucks, etc.

- The following are more examples you may wish to introduce: the temperature is high in the summer and low in the winter; when we go to the circus, we watch the trapeze artists fly high in the air, while the elephants walk low to the ground; skyscrapers stand high in the sky, and houses are low to the ground.

- Have the children stand up high, then bend down low.

- For Trolley Stop Activity 17O, the children will color the child who is reaching up high. Next, the children will put an X on the child who is bending down low.

Trolley Stop Activity 17O

Readiness Lane
Preschool Readiness Activities

Trolley Stop Activity 17P

14. TOP and BOTTOM

- Take turns measuring how tall a child is from the top of his/her head to the bottom of his/her feet.
- On the playground, fill a container up to the top with sand, then dump it out so you can see the bottom.
- On the playground, take turns climbing to the top of the slide and sliding down to the bottom.
- Point to objects around the room (eraser, basket, desk, etc.) and have children identify the top and bottom of each item.
- For Trolley Stop Activity 17P, the children will draw a child at the top of the slide. Next, the children will make a mud puddle at the bottom of the slide.

Trolley Stop Activity 17Q

15. HAPPY and SAD

- Ask the children to describe how they feel when they are happy and when they are sad.
- With the children, make a list on the board or on chart paper of things that might make the children feel happy. Next, make a list of things that might make the children feel sad.
- Choose volunteers to act as if they were happy; sad.
- Look for pictures in magazines, etc. that depict a variety of facial expressions. Use these pictures for an oral language lesson: "Does the girl in the picture look happy? Why?"
- For Trolley Stop Activity 17Q, have the children make one clown look sad, and the other clown look happy. Discuss with the children how they knew which clown to pick (one clown has curved eyebrows).

16. WIDE and NARROW

- Find or draw a picture on the board of a wide street and a narrow street. Ask the children to identify which one is wide and which is narrow. Why?
- Let all the children open their eyes wide, then their mouths.
- Identify with the children a wide doorway or entryway and a narrow one if available. Invite them to walk through the wide doorway and the narrow doorway.

HANDS-ON ACTIVITIES TO LEARN OPPOSITES Continued

- Paint a wide stripe with a paintbrush. Next, paint a narrow strip with another paintbrush. Choose volunteers to paint a wide stripe and a narrow stripe.
- For Trolley Stop Activity 17R, the children will draw a car on the wide street, and a bicycle on the narrow street.

Trolley Stop Activity 17R

17. FAST and SLOW

- Find and cut out a variety of transportation pictures (cars, trucks, bicycles, airplanes, etc.) and have the children tell you which ones go "fast" and which ones go "slow".
- Ask the children to walk around the room fast, then slow; run around the room fast, then slow; skip around the room fast, then slow; hop around the room fast, then slow; etc.
- Give the children a sentence to say fast, then slow.
- Draw or find pictures of a tricycle, car, airplane, train, and space shuttle, and help the children sequence them going from the slowest (tricycle) to the fastest (space shuttle). You may wish to extend this activity to another category: animals.
- For Trolley Stop Activity 17S, the children will color the animal that is slow (turtle). Next, the children will color the object that goes the fastest (airplane).

Trolley Stop Activity 17S

18. SOFT and HARD

- Let the children take turns sitting in a hard chair, then a soft chair (you may bring in a cushion or pillow if there are no "soft" chairs).
- Compare carpet and concrete, clay and crayons, etc. Which one is soft? Which one is hard?
- Make a "mystery" bag with soft and hard items. Suggestions for soft items: feather, cotton, scraps of velvet, sponge ball, carpet scraps, etc. Suggestions for hard items: plastic box, pencil, button, spoon, block, etc.
- For Trolley Stop Activity 17T, the children will draw a cat in the chair that is soft. Next, the children will draw an X on the seat that is hard.

Trolley Stop Activity 17T

HANDS-ON ACTIVITIES TO LEARN OPPOSITES Continued

19. NOISY and QUIET

Trolley Stop Activity 17U

- Have the children practice being "quiet," with hands in their laps and not saying anything. Then have them practice being "noisy" by clapping their hands, jumping up and down, etc.
- Look for pictures that represent noisy and quiet and help the children categorize them.
- Give each child a musical instrument to play, i.e. drum, triangle, sandpaper blocks, etc. Let all the children with drums practice being noisy while the others practice being quiet. Make sure everyone gets a turn to practice being noisy!
- For Trolley Stop Activity 17U, the children will circle the child who is quiet. Next, the children will color the child who is noisy.

20. STOP and GO

Trolley Stop Activity 17V

- Introduce this concept by asking the children to move around the room when you say "go," and to freeze in place when you say "stop."
- Talk about traffic lights and the color green that means "go," and the color red that means "stop." You may also wish to talk about cars needing fuel to run ("go") and what happens when they run out of fuel ("stop").
- Teach hand signals for "stop" and "go" and let the children pretend they are directing traffic.
- For Trolley Stop Activity 17V, the children will color the car that is going, and draw a circle around the car that is stopped.

21. INSIDE and OUTSIDE

Trolley Stop Activity 17W

- Make a square with masking tape on the floor. Choose volunteers to step inside the square, then step outside the square. This activity may be played outside on concrete using chalk.
- Gather items that would usually belong inside (pencil, paper, book, etc.), and items that would usually belong or be used outside (umbrella, coat, tricycle, beach ball, etc.) Help the children classify them.
- For Trolley Stop Activity 17W, the children will draw an X on the bird that is <u>inside</u> the birdhouse. Next, the children will color the bird that is <u>outside</u> the birdhouse.

HANDS-ON ACTIVITIES TO LEARN OPPOSITES Continued

22. MANY and FEW

- On chart paper, draw a small square to represent a house and a large rectangle to represent a skyscraper (be sure to talk about what a skyscraper is). Take turns pasting or drawing squares ("windows") on the house and the skyscraper. There are a "few" windows on the house, but there are "many" windows on the skyscraper.

- Repeat the activity described above with a variety of examples: car/bus, airplane/helicopter, apartment building/ ice cream store.

- Let the children collect leaves, nuts, etc. from the playground. Provide different-sized containers or boxes to store the items. Talk about which containers hold many items, and which store only a few.

- For Trolley Stop Activity 17X, the children will draw an X on the road with many cars. The children will not draw anything on the road with a few cars.

- Move the Trolley to the next stop on the Jolly Trolley Chart.

Trolley Stop Activity 17X

Once the children have come this far in learning about opposites, you may want to add to the list. Additional examples are:

- awake and asleep
- day and night
- light and dark
- tall and short
- wet and dry
- hot and cold
- dirty and clean
- lost and found
- heavy and light
- hello and good-bye
- lose and win
- summer and winter
- work and play

- black and white
- tight and loose
- empty and full
- young and old
- fat and thin
- push and pull
- come and go
- here and there
- near and far
- to and from
- thick and thin
- loud and soft

14 HANDS-ON ACTIVITIES TO LEARN DIRECTIONAL CONCEPTS

Trolley Stop Activities 18A-J

Objective

To provide hands on, motivational group and individual experiences and activities to guide preschool children to learn to recognize the directional concepts:

- next to
- between
- through
- left and right

1. NEXT TO

Trolley Stop Activity 18A

- Take turns having two children stand next to each other.
- Pick objects from around the room and give each child an opportunity to tell what any one of those objects is next to.
- Choose several children to form a line and ask, "Who is next to the last in line?"
- Have children identify the pictures for Next To, Trolley Stop Activity 18A. Then, have the children put a face on the child next to the teacher.

2. BETWEEN

Trolley Stop Activity 18B

- Have three children stand in front of the room; name the child who is in between.
- Practice with objects from around the room. For example: put a block between two other blocks, put a book on the shelf that is between the top shelf and the bottom shelf.
- Draw two squares on the board; ask a child to draw a circle between them.
- Form a circle and have the children stand with their legs apart. Choose a child to stand in the middle of the circle and roll the ball between another child's legs. Have the two children exchange places and repeat.
- Following the directions for Trolley Stop Activity 18B, the children will draw a cat between two trees, and a girl between two boys.

Readiness Lane
Preschool Readiness Activities

HANDS-ON ACTIVITIES TO LEARN DIRECTIONAL CONCEPTS Continued

3. THROUGH

- Tell the children to run their fingers through their hair.
- Ask a child to walk through the doorway.
- On the playground, have the children pretend they are birds flying through the air, then driving through a tunnel.
- Have students identify and color the picture of the beads with the string going <u>through</u> them for Trolley Stop Activity 18C.
- You may wish to have the children practice stringing real beads.

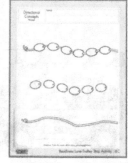

Trolley Stop Activity 18C

4. LEFT TO RIGHT

The following are activities that should be continued all year because this concept is difficult for young children. If some children continue to get mixed up, don't worry; they will get a lot more practice in kindergarten. Remember always - no pressure.

- Tie a piece of yarn on the children's right wrists or ankles and leave them there all day or all week. (Bracelets may also be made out of construction paper.)
- Tell the children, "This is the right hand which we hold over our hearts when we pledge to our flag."
- Play "Simon Says": "Simon Says to shake your left foot; Simon Says to wiggle the fingers of your right hand; Simon Says to hold your left arm high; Simon Says to wink your right eye; Simon Says to pull your left ear," etc.

LOOBY LOO SONG

Play "Looby Loo," on Cassette or CD, emphasizing <u>left</u> and <u>right</u>. "Looby Loo" Lyrics in Music section, TM p. 69.

- Let the children draw pictures: "Put a house on the <u>left</u>, a tree on the <u>right</u>," etc.
- There are seven "left to right" activities, Trolley Stop Activities 18D to 18J. Follow the directions for each activity.
- Move the trolley to the next stop on the Jolly Trolley Chart.

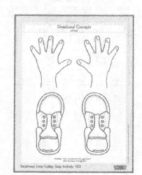

Trolley Stop Activity 18D

4 HANDS-ON ACTIVITIES TO LEARN CLASSIFICATION

Trolley Stop Activities 19A-F

Objective

To provide hands-on, motivational group and individual experiences and activities to guide preschool children to learn to:

- identify and classify pictures into categories

Recommended Read Aloud Literature

In A People House by Theo. LeSieg

Things That Go! By Anne Rockwell

Rosie Rabbit Goes To Preschool by Patrick Yee

There are four types of stores presented in this section: a toy store, clothing store, furniture store, and grocery store.

- Talk about ways to classify children into two groups and then practice. For example: boys and girls, long hair and short hair, sneakers or sandals, etc.

- Give each child a picture of a person or an animal. The children holding a picture of a person will sit together, and the children holding a picture of an animal will sit together.

- Gather familiar toys from around the room (blocks, trucks, dolls, crayons, etc.). Next, gather objects from an unrelated category such as kitchen/lunch room objects (spoon, plate, cup, napkin, thermos, etc.). Help the children decide which objects belong in the toy chest, and which objects belong in the kitchen/lunch room. Categories may be changed for more practice and variety.

Readiness Lane
Preschool Readiness Activities

HANDS-ON ACTIVITIES TO LEARN CLASSIFICATION Continued

- Select a storefront bulletin board of your choice (examples: candy store, drug store, book store, pet store, restaurant, etc.). Have the children draw or cut out pictures from magazines to tack up on the storefront that sells those items.

- Set up a workbench with tools; a "house" with furnishings; a "farm" with animals; a "zoo" with animals, etc.

- For Trolley Stop Activities 19A to 19C, talk about the types of stores presented: **toy store** and **clothing store**. The children will cut out items and paste each on the store in which it belongs.

- Follow the procedure described above for Trolley Stop Activities 19D to 19F. The children will cut out items and paste each on the store in which it belongs (**furniture store** or **grocery store**).

- Move the trolley to the next stop on the Jolly Trolley Chart.

Trolley Stop Activity 19A

Trolley Stop Activities 19B, 19C, 19E and 19F

Sing Spell Read&Write.

8 HANDS-ON ACTIVITIES TO LEARN SEQUENCING

<u>Trolley Stop Activities</u> 20A-H

<u>Objective</u>

To provide hands-on, motivational group and individual experiences and activities to guide preschool children to learn to:

- place story pictures in sequence

<u>Recommended Read Aloud Literature</u>

The Carrot Seed by Ruth Krauss
Growing Vegetable Soup by Lois Ehlert
Peanut Butter and Jelly, A Play Rhyme by Nadine Bernard Westcott

There are eight Sequence Stories in this section:

1. **Brushing Your Teeth**
2. **Sliding Board**
3. **Blowing Bubbles**
4. **Planting A Flower**
5. **Washing Your Hands**
6. **Changing A Flat Tire**
7. **Writing and Mailing a Letter**
8. **Birds Building a Nest/Hatching Eggs**

- Brainstorm with the children what they do each morning upon their arrival at school, i.e. hang up jacket, put lunchbox away, have story time, play outside, etc.

Trolley Stop Activities 20A-20H:
Sequence Stories 1-8

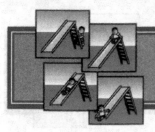

HANDS-ON ACTIVITIES TO LEARN SEQUENCING Continued

- Call on a child to tell "what happened first," on another child to tell "what happened next," etc. Focus the attention on achieving the proper sequence.

- You may wish to make a book telling about what a typical school day is like and display it for parents to read.

- Give the children other opportunities to practice sequencing, i.e. retelling a familiar or favorite story (in sequence), sequencing a familiar or favorite story with pictures, etc.

- Help children cut out pictures for Sequence Story 1 (brushing teeth), Trolley Stop Activity 20A, and arrange them in sequential order.

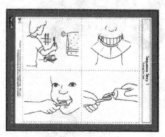

Trolley Stop Activity 20A
Sequence Story 1

- Children will paste the pictures on a sheet of paper in proper left-to-right order, or staple to make storybooks with them.

- Have children color the pictures.

- Give children the opportunity to tell their own personal stories with the pictures.

- As the children become more experienced at sequencing, they may number some pictures in sequence right on the page.

- Continue in the same manner for Sequence Stories 2-8, Trolley Stop Activities 20B to 20H.

- For more practice in sequencing, old magazines or discarded storybooks may be cut up, arranged in sequential order, pasted on paper, and made into a book.

- Move the trolley to the next stop on the Jolly Trolley Chart.

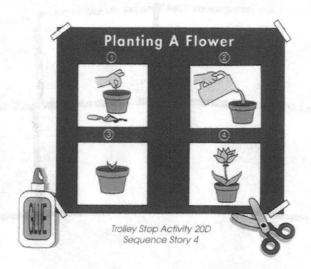

Trolley Stop Activity 20D
Sequence Story 4

Readiness Lane
Preschool Readiness Activities

5 HANDS-ON ACTIVITIES TO LEARN SEASONS

Trolley Stop Activities 21A-E

Objective

To provide hands-on, motivational group and individual experiences and activities to guide preschool children to learn to become familiar with:
- the seasons of the year
- matching seasonal clothing to the weather
- dressing skills

Recommended Read Aloud Literature

The Mitten by Jan Brett

Touch and Feel Clothes by DK Publishing, Inc.

In the Rain with Baby Duck by Amy Hest

A Summer Picnic by Richard Scarry

My Spring Robin by Anne Rockwell

Snow by Roy McKie and P.D. Eastman

A Little Bit of Winter by Paul Stewart

Animals should definitely <u>not</u> wear clothing. by Judi Barrett

The Seasons of Arnold's Apple Tree by Gail Gibbons

The Teddy Bears' Picnic by Jimmy Kennedy

Introducing the Seasons

- Spend a minimum of one day introducing each season: **spring, summer, fall,** and **winter.** Talk about what typically occurs during each season. For example, in fall, leaves turn colors and fall to the ground, birds fly south, squirrels gather nuts and bury them, some animals get ready to hibernate, etc. Pictures, stories, poems, etc. will greatly enhance your discussions.

- Divide a piece of chart paper or poster board into four equal boxes. Draw a picture of a tree as it would look in **spring** (blossoms are budding). Next, draw the same tree over again as it would appear in **summer** (full of green leaves). Then, draw the tree over again as it would appear in **fall** (colored leaves falling to ground). For the final picture, draw the tree as it would appear in **winter** (no leaves, maybe some snow on the branches). Label each picture with the appropriate season as you talk about what has happened to the same tree at different times of the year. Display the pictures so they may be a frame of reference.

- Have the children draw a picture of something they like to do during the season you are studying.

Readiness Lane
Preschool Readiness Activities

HANDS-ON ACTIVITIES TO LEARN SEASONS Continued

Once all of the seasons have been introduced, you will want to be sure to talk about **weather patterns** for each season.

- You may wish to keep a weather calendar. Choose a different child each day to draw a picture of a sun, rain, wind, clouds, or snow in the square by that day's date. (Be sure your calendar has large enough squares to accommodate a child's drawing.)

- Choose a different child each day to be "weatherperson."

- On chart paper, make a list with the children's input of things to do on a rainy day, sunny day, etc. Let each child choose one to illustrate.

- Gather clothing representing the different seasons as well as weather patterns: bathing suit, hat, gloves/mittens, scarf, raincoat, boots, baseball hat, jacket, coat, t-shirt, shorts, sweatshirt, etc. The children will be more familiar with some clothing than others, so be sure to hold each item up and name it.

- Ask the children what they would choose to wear on a rainy day, with a volunteer choosing the appropriate piece(s) of clothing from the pile. Repeat the exercise, asking what the children would wear on a windy day, etc.

- Make a bulletin board with pictures of all the different clothes that can be worn during that time of year.

- Make a class scrapbook with pictures of children and grown-ups dressed for each of the seasons.

- Discuss with the children the seasons of the year that the pictures for Trolley Stop Activities 21A and 21B depict (winter, spring).

- Direct the children to draw a big green X on all the clothes the boy and girl should be wearing while playing in the snow.

- Next, tell the children to draw an orange circle around the clothing the children should wear as they go out in the rain.

Trolley Stop Activity 21A
Winter

Trolley Stop Activity 21B
Spring

Sing Spell Read & Write

HANDS-ON ACTIVITIES TO LEARN SEASONS Continued

Trolley Stop Activity 21C

- On Trolley Stop Activities 21C and 21D, discuss with the children the seasons of the year that the pictures depict. (fall, summer)
- Direct the children to underline everything the boy and girl will need going to school on a spring morning.
- Next, have the children cut out the things that might be used for swimming.
- The children may paste the items where they wish on the picture.
- Move the trolley to the next stop on the Jolly Trolley Chart.

DRESSING SKILLS

Trolley Stop Activity 21D

- Create a dress-up corner in the room. Let the children pick appropriate clothes to dress in while the others guess for which weather they are dressed.
- On Trolley Stop Activity 21E, there is a check-off list of clothing that the children should know how to put on/take off. For example, when the children are able to zip or button their coats or jackets a few times, check them off.
- If you care to do it at this time, help the children learn to tie their shoes. Use the shoe with real lace on the manipulative provided.

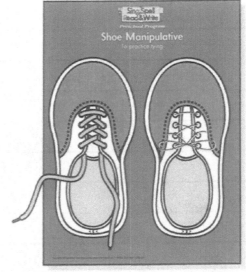

Shoe Manipulative

Trolley Stop Activity 21E

NOTES

OVERVIEW OF ACTIVITIES

The activities along **Alphabet Lane** introduce preschool children to
- phonemic awareness (conscious awareness of speech sounds)
- letter names and sounds (phonics)

Four activities are presented for each letter of the alphabet A to Z.

1. SING ALONG PHONICS SONG ACTIVITIES

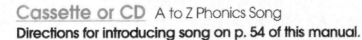

(Join the Dots...What is it?)

Trolley Stop Activities A1 to Z1

Cassette or CD A to Z Phonics Song
Directions for introducing song on p. 54 of this manual.

These activities present a **KEY WORD PHONICS PICTURE** for children to
1. **TRACE** dot-to-dot
2. **SAY** the **NAME** of the object
3. **IDENTIFY** the **BEGINNING SOUND** of the object
4. **LEARN** the **NAME** and **SOUND** of the **LETTER**
5. **COLOR** the picture
6. **PARENTAL COMPONENT:** take pictures home, sing and point from A to Z for parents.

DIRECTIONS:

- Tell the children we are going to be doing an activity every day, and that the activities will get them ready to read by teaching them about the letters of the alphabet...Aren't all books and signs made up of lots of letters that *say* something? The more we know about the letters, the better we will be able to read! And we are going to start today! Tell the children they should save their **A to Z Phonics Song Pictures** daily as they can be hung on the wall at home as a **SING ALONG AND POINT SET** (just like the ones on the bulletin board at school). Be sure to tell them to ask Mom or Dad where they may hang them!

SING ALONG PHONICS SONG ACTIVITIES Continued

- Next, tell children to put their pencil point or crayon in the "start" dot, and go the way the arrow points tracing over the dotted line. Then ask someone to tell what they see a picture of. "Apple!" Yes! Then, tell them to look at the letters below the apple, and ask if anyone can tell you what these two letters are. "Letters **Aa!**" Yes! We call them **A**'s...and continue: Do you know that each one of those **A**'s, the big (capital) one, and the small (lower case) one has a SOUND that it makes? And to find out the sound, we have to say the name of the Key Word. Let's say it together...apple. Now, let's say it again and just say the beginning of the word, and see if we can get the sound of letter **A**. (Say ăăăăăăpple, stretching out the first sound of the word.) The sound of letter **A** is ăăăă! Let's point to the big letter **A** and say "ăăă," then point to the little letter **A** and say ăăă, then point to the picture of the apple and say **"apple!"** Teacher: Ă, ă, ăpple. **Children: Ă, ă, ăpple!**

- Follow the 1, 2, 3 as designated on the Activity, pointing and saying sounds. **Finally, sum it up for them: This is an A and it says Ă (pointing)...This is small letter a, and it says ă also, (pointing), and this is an apple (pointing). Apple starts with the ă sound.**

This is the format for introducing all SING ALONG PHONICS SONG (JOIN THE DOTS...WHAT IS IT?) ACTIVITIES.

2. POINT, SAY, AND COLOR ACTIVITIES
Trolley Stop Activities A2 to Z2

POINT, SAY, AND COLOR ACTIVITIES present pictured items which start with the key letter sound. Children are to name the pictured items (with help from the teacher) and listen to the beginning sounds. Next, have children point to

- (1) the capital letter and say its sound
- (2) the small letter and say its sound
- (3) the pictured items and name them

Trolley Stop Activity A2

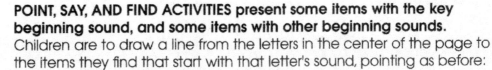

POINT, SAY, AND COLOR ACTIVITIES Continued

EACH TIME, POINT TO LETTERS FIRST AND SAY SOUNDS: "Ă, ă, ănt, "Ă, ă, ăddress, Ă, ă, ănger," etc., around the page. Then have children color the pictures.

Follow this format for all POINT, SAY, AND COLOR ACTIVITIES.

Trolley Stop Activity A3

3. POINT, SAY, AND FIND ACTIVITIES

Trolley Stop Activities A3 to Z3

POINT, SAY, AND FIND ACTIVITIES present some items with the key beginning sound, and some items with other beginning sounds.
Children are to draw a line from the letters in the center of the page to the items they find that start with that letter's sound, pointing as before:

    (1) first to capital letter, saying its sound

    (2) then to little letter, saying its sound

    (3) then to the items, going around the page: Ă, ă, ăccident, Ă, ă, ăthlete, but not Ă, ă, music.

Follow this format for all POINT, SAY, AND FIND ACTIVITIES.

Trolley Stop Activity A4

4. FOLLOWING DIRECTIONS ACTIVITIES

Trolley Stop Activities A4 to Z4

FOLLOWING DIRECTIONS ACTIVITIES present a picture of an item with the key beginning sound for the children to color. In addition, the children may be asked to draw a specified item with the key beginning sound to "complete" the picture.

Follow this format for all FOLLOWING DIRECTIONS ACTIVITIES.

MANIPULATIVES

1. CLOCK

    A clock with moving hour hand will help the young children learn to tell time on the hour.

2. ALPH-O PUZZLES

    There are sets of A to Z letter puzzles. Keep the puzzle pieces in baggies, no more than 4 letter puzzles per baggie for young children. The children will enjoy putting the puzzles together in their free "choosing" time, matching capital and small letters.

 **Alphabet Lane**
Preschool Readiness Activities

MANIPULATIVES Continued

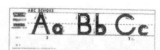

3. A TO Z MANUSCRIPT WALL CARDS**

Children will sing along and point to wall cards for learning **names** of letters A to Z. (Traditional Alphabet Song on Cassette/CD)

** *In classroom program only*

4. PLACEMAT: JOLLY TROLLEY CHART
ALPHABET LANE SONG/PICTURES (side 1)
A TO Z PHONICS SONG (side 2)

Sing along and point placemat for individual practice as the child learns the names and sounds of the letters A to Z.

Placemat Side 1

5. ABC STRIP (side 1)/NUMBER LINE (side 2)

Children sing along and point on ABC Strip for ABC Song (traditional), and learn about numbers 0 to 10.

Placemat Side 2

Phonemic Awareness Games

- After children have completed the four activities for each letter, tell them they may play a listening game. Then say three words aloud, two of which use the beginning sound that has just been studied; i.e., "apple, telephone, ax." Let a child tell which two words start with the same beginning sound. Tell which word does not start with the same sound.

Sing Along and Point Strip - Side 1

Number Line - Side 2

- Tell children you are going to say some words, and when they hear one that starts with a different beginning sound, they should clap their hands. Then say "ball, bat, boy, box, zebra **(clap)** bed, bench," etc. This game gives the children excellent practice in hearing the beginning sounds.

- When a few letters have been taught, write one of these letters on the board. Let a child volunteer to give its sound. This may be done with all the letters that have been previously taught.

Alph-O Game

- Distribute the Alph-O cards, **letter side up**, one to each child. Choose one child to stand up and show his or her letter. Let others volunteer to give the sound of the letter. After a correct sound has been given, the child standing may point to another child, who will stand and hold up his or her card. The children will love singing, "Here We Go 'Round The Alphabet" each time a new leader is chosen.

HERE WE GO 'ROUND THE ALPHABET
(Tune: The Mulberry Bush)
"Here we go 'round the alphabet,
Here we go 'round the alphabet,
Here we go 'round the alphabet,
Who will stand up next?"

Picture Side   Letter Side

Alph-O Game Continued

Picture Side   Letter Side

- The game may also be played **picture side up**. Let the volunteer give the beginning sound.

- Place Alph-O Cards down on a table, **letter side up**. Let children take turns choosing a card, giving its sound, and saying a word that begins with that sound. Next, play the game with picture side up. Have the children either give the beginning sound, or name another object that starts with that sound.

ALPHABET LANE SONG

Goal: To sing together **daily** to introduce names and sounds of letters A to Z.

Directions:

Cassette or CD Alphabet Lane Song
Lyrics in Music section, TM p. 70

- Invite the children to sit on a carpet in front of the Jolly Trolley Chart for close up seeing/pointing/touching and discussion. You will be concentrating on the **Alphabet Lane** portion of the chart.

- Begin listening to the **Alphabet Lane Song**. Locate the section on Alphabet Lane for Letter Aa and point along as the children sing: "A says ă, do you hear it in apple?"

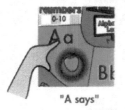
"A says"

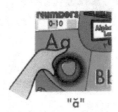
"ă"

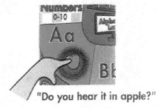
"Do you hear it in apple?"

- Continue in this way through the song for letters B to Z, pointing first to the capital letter, then to the small letter, and then to the key word phonics picture for each letter along Alphabet Lane.

- After singing the song several times, ask if anyone would like to be leader and point the way you did.

- When children feel comfortable singing and pointing along to the wall chart, they are ready to sing along and point using the **Jolly Trolley Chart Placemats**.

Jolly Trolley Chart Placemat

ABC Alphabet Lane
Preschool Readiness Activities

A TO Z PHONICS SONG

Goal: To sing together as a group the A to Z Phonics Song **each day** as the children learn about the letters A to Z

Directions:

Cassette or CD A to Z Phonics Song
Sheet Music in Music section, TM pp. 71-72

- Place the alphabet picture cards (apple, ball, cat, etc.)** in rows on a bulletin board, preferably with a carpet in front for children to sit on for close-up seeing/pointing/ touching and discussion. There are numbers on these cards to help you place them in their position, so look for the tiny #1 on the bottom of the first card to begin.
  ** *In classroom program only*

- Begin listening to the A to Z Phonics Song:

  "When we learn these sounds you'll see,
  Ready to read then we will be"

- Now point to the wall card with the apple, first pointing to capital **A**, then to little **a**, then to the picture of the **apple**, as the children sing:

" Ă, ă, ăpple"

- Then point to capital **B**, then to little **b**, then to the picture of the ball, as the children sing:

"bh, bh, ball"

- Continue in this way through the song, **pointing first to the capital letter, then to the small letter, and then to the picture, for each card from A to Z.** Your pointer will really be moving along to keep up with the music! *Don't point to each word on the cards with words only.* After learning the song well, you will probably turn to look at the class when you come to these cards.

A TO Z PHONICS SONG Continued

- After singing the song several times, ask if anyone in the room thinks he or she can be the leader and point the way you did:

  > first to the capital letter,
  > then to the small letter,
  > then to the picture, for each card across the room.

- Ask the children to be very careful to say the sounds the way they are on the cassette/CD and not to add an "ŭ" sound with each sound they sing! This takes practice to do properly and is very important.

- Teach sound of "**x**" at the end of words as "ks" (bo**x**, si**x**, etc.).

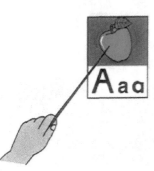

- After choosing someone to be the leader, tell the children they must keep their eyes at the tip of the pointer while singing this song. Tell them that the children who learn to read the best always keep their eyes at the tip of the pointer when singing this song. You might add, "Let's see how many good readers we're going to have this year!" If you will compliment a few children for watching carefully, you'll see how the rest start watching carefully too. This is extremely important! **To sing without looking is a total waste of time. Insist! This is Auditory-Visual training, both hearing the sound and seeing the shapes of the letters that make the sound. So Sing and Listen, and Look and Point!**

- When the children feel comfortable singing and pointing with the wall cards, they are ready to sing along and point individually using the **A to Z Phonics Song Placemats**.

ABC SONG (traditional)

Goal: To sing together **daily** as a group to introduce and learn names of letters A to Z.

Teacher: Note different pauses to eliminate "LMNOP":
A B C D E F G H I J K L M N – O P Q R S T U – V – W X Y Z
Now I know my ABC's, next time won't you sing with me?

Directions:
<u>Cassette or CD</u> ABC Song (traditional)
Sing to the tune of *Twinkle, Twinkle Little Star*

- Display wall cards (in classroom program only) in rows on wall, preferably with a carpet in front for children to sit on for close up seeing and pointing.

- Have children take turns pointing to letters as the group sings along!

Sing Along and Point Alphabet Strip

- Distribute individual Alphabet Strip to each child to sing along and point to the letters of the alphabet.

Along ***Alphabet Lane*** there are four "Musical Math Houses" to indicate where the children will learn (through songs and activities) about numbers 0-10.

Math activities are introduced:

After letter **D** at **Math House #1** -See TM p. 57
After letter **H** at **Math House #2** -See TM p. 63
After letter **L** at **Math House #3** -See TM p. 63
After letter **P** at **Math House #4** -See TM p. 64

OVERVIEW

By the time children are age two or three, parents have usually taught them "rote" counting, which means they "recite" the number words "one, two, three, etc." without attaching any meaning to them. Later, children learn "rational counting," which means they begin to be able to count objects in a group. In this stage they start developing a "connection" between the number "symbols" (numerals) and the number words they are "reciting." They begin to get a basic understanding of the use of numbers.

Children learn that:

- The symbol "1" is called "one" and means one item;
- The symbol "2" is called "two" and means two items;
- The symbol "3" is called "three" and means three items, etc.

Parents and teachers can help children develop the number concept by having them begin to count objects early on: beans, spoons, pennies, peanuts, M&Ms, cars (anything!). This will help children start making the connection between number words, symbols, and their meaning. **Beginners should touch items as they count them, remembering to say just one number per touch.**

Recommended Read Aloud Literature

I'll Teach My Dog 100 Words by Michael Frith

Ten Apples Up On Top! by Theo. LeSieg

One Fish, Two Fish, Red Fish, Blue Fish by Dr. Seuss

Goldilocks and The Three Bears retold and illustrated by Jan Brett

MATH READINESS LESSON #1:
Why Do We Have To Learn About Numbers?

Visit Musical Math House #1
Next to letter D on Alphabet Lane

Cassette or CD Song– "Why Do We Have to Learn About Numbers?"

Math Readiness
Preschool Readiness Activities

ACTIVITIES

- Listen to song (on cassette or CD) "Why Do We Have to Learn About Numbers?" Discuss with the children the reasons they heard in the song for learning numbers.
- Have children draw or cut out pictures showing everyday life activities for which we must use and know numbers.

SONG LYRICS:

Child: Teacher, why do we have to learn about numbers?

Teacher: Why, Bobby, there are lots of reasons why we have to learn about numbers. Listen to this song and we will learn why.

Singer:
There are so many numbers
We'll surely have to learn.
So many, many numbers
They're everywhere you turn.

On license plates and houses
On all things in the store.
So many, many, many numbers!
Perhaps one billion or more!

Child 1:
Like numbers on my telephone
My radio and TV
Numbers on my microwave
And on the bus you'll see.

Child 2:
There are numbers on all paper money
Dimes and nickels too.
Numbers on the highway signs
And on that plane we flew.

Child 3:
There are numbers on the pages
Of magazines and books.
Numbers on the calculators
Where my daddy works.

SONG LYRICS Continued

"Why Do We Have to Learn About Numbers?"

Child 4:	Numbers on my ruler-and-scale, Oh, it's clear to me! That I must learn numbers For a happy life for me.
All:	That I must learn numbers For a happy life for me.
Teacher:	Good! Now let's slow down a bit and see who can think of some questions someone might ask that could be answered with numbers. Think about it!

Child 1:	How many children, moms and dads?
Child 2:	How many kittens all of them had?
Child 3:	How many houses, schools and farms?
Child 4:	How many puppies fit in your arms?
Child 1:	How many airplanes? How many boats?
Child 2:	How many hats and how many coats?
Child 3:	How many people? How many chairs?
Child 4:	How many plums and how many pears?

Child 1:	How many trees and flowers and kites?
Child 2:	How many days and how many nights? All of our lives we have to count, And that's what numbers are all about.
All:	Yes, all of our lives we have to count, And that's what numbers are all about.
Teacher:	Good! What are some other questions That are answered with numbers? All the ones you named started with "how many". Can you think of some others?

Child 1:	What time is it now? How far did we go?
Child 2:	How much are the tickets? How long is the show?

SONG LYRICS Continued

"Why Do We Have to Learn About Numbers?"

Child 3:   How big is the room?
             What size is the rug?

Child 4:   How big are these shoes?
             This size is too snug!

Child 1:   How big is the cake?
             How many candles?

Child 2:   How many bicycles
             With tassels on their handles?

Child 3:   How tall is the building?
             How large are the cities?

Child 4:   We'll have to know numbers
             To answer these ditties.

Teacher: But numbers are easy
             If you learn with songs.

Teacher &
Child 1:   They'll teach what we need
             So we'll never be wrong.

All: Just sing-along now
             Learn to count and to add
             To "take-away" too,
             And we'll be very glad.

             (Yes) Musical Math Facts
             Are fun as can be!
             Our own calculators
             We soon will be!

             (Yes) Musical Math Facts
             Are fun as can be!
             Our own calculators
             We soon will be!

Teacher: So that's why we're learning about numbers!
All: OK, let's learn!

The Story of WHERE NUMBERS CAME FROM

Introducing the Numbers 1 to 10

To the Teacher:

This is the story script about the "invention" of numbers. You will want to use the counting sticks included in the kit to help the children get a concrete concept of the symbol. Suggestion: Use velcro or magnets on counting sticks.

STORY SCRIPT FOR NUMBER "1"

"Once upon a time, long, long ago, a cave man used one stick or one finger to represent "1". The cave man used it to mean one child, one leaf, one dog, one bird, one cave, one tree, and so on." Write the symbol "1" on paper or the chalkboard and show the children that it looks like that number 1 "stick" the cave man used to mean "one".

STORY SCRIPT FOR NUMBER "2"

Next teach "2". Tell the story of the cave man who invented "2" by showing two fingers held sideways,

or by 2 sticks like this, demonstrating with counting sticks. Then say, "I think I will join those two sticks together to make the numeral two! He used a piece of vine to do it." (Draw the vine between the sticks.)

"See the numeral 2?" Next, identify groups of two: 2 hands, 2 feet, 2 eyes, 2 children, 2 crayons, etc. To practice the concept of "2", have the children make two large circles on paper and draw two items in each (2 dots, 2 stars, 2 hearts, etc.)

STORY SCRIPT FOR NUMBER "3"

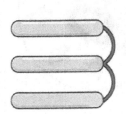

Tell the children how the cave man would use 3 fingers or 3 sticks as shown. Then tell how he joined the sticks with the vines to make numeral "3". Have the children draw groups of 3 items in circles on paper. The idea in these lessons is to help the children see the abstract symbols (1,2,3,etc.) as concrete "evidence" of the number they represent (with the correct number of "sticks" joined together). This serves as a bridge from the concrete (counting sticks or fingers) to the abstract symbols.

STORY SCRIPT Continued

STORY SCRIPT FOR NUMBER "4"

Next, teach 4. Use counting sticks to form 4, and tell the cave man story as you did when teaching 1, 2, and 3. "Once there was a cave man who wanted to make a 4, so he placed 4 sticks together like this: One day the wind blew and a stick fell over, so sometimes you see *four* this way." (See fig. B)

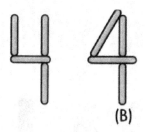

(B)

STORY SCRIPT FOR NUMBER "5"

Next, teach 5. Tell the cave man story showing the 5 sticks used to make "5".

It looks very much like today's computer "5"! The children will see the "concrete evidence" that 5 is made of 5 sticks.

REVIEW PRACTICE TIME

Write any number on a paper or chart. Have the children place the correct number of items next to the numerals.

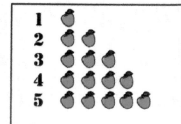

TEACHING NUMBERS 6-10

We have gone as far as we can go with our "cave man sticks" "abstract-to-concrete story", but continue to introduce numbers 6 to 10. Have children draw circles on paper and fill them in with the specified number of items (stars, dots, etc.) for each number.

MATH READINESS LESSON #2:
Counting to Ten Song

Visit Musical Math House #2
Next to Letter H on Alphabet Lane

Cassette or CD "Counting to Ten Song"

ACTIVITIES

- Draw a number line 1-10 on the board or on a paper roll with numbers six inches apart. Sing along and point with the music.
- Distribute Number Lines and have children point along to numbers as they sing the "Counting to Ten" song.
- At this time, present the CLOCK MANIPULATIVE. Introduce the hour hand and talk about "o'clock." Practice counting around the clock with the hour hand and saying "1 o'clock, 2 o'clock," etc.

MATH READINESS LESSON #3:
"Counting Backwards Song"

Visit Musical Math House #3
Next to Letter L on Alphabet Lane

Cassette or CD "Counting Backwards Song" (10 to 1)

ACTIVITIES

- Draw a number line 1 to 10 on the board or on a paper roll with numbers six inches apart. Sing along and point with the music.
- Distribute Number Lines and have children point along to numbers as they sing the "Counting Backwards" song.

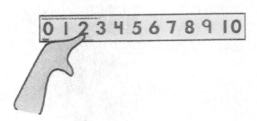

Math Readiness
Preschool Readiness Activities

MATH READINESS LESSON #4: ZERO SONG

Visit Musical Math House #4
Next to Letter P on Alphabet Lane

Cassette or CD "The Zero Song"

SONG LYRICS:

Zeros, zeros, zeros
Zeros all around.
Nothing, nothing, nothing,
Nothing can be found.

When we're adding zeros
It is like a game
Yes, when we add a zero
The number stays the same.

ACTIVITIES

- Introduce the concept of zero using the word "nothing".
- Have the children form a circle facing inward. Show them how to "make" a zero with their arms by holding their hands clasped over their heads.
- When the lyrics of the song say "zero", the children will make this motion.
- When the lyrics say "nothing, nothing, nothing", the children will show empty palms, rotating wrists.
- When the lyrics say each number in turn, they are to show that number of fingers.
- Optional: On the choruses, children may turn and skip following one another in a circle around the room. Have fun!

Colors Song
(Point along to pictures on Jolly Trolley Chart as children sing)

(Verse 1)   RED and YELLOW
BLUE and GREEN
ORANGE, PURPLE, BROWN
BLACK and PINK and
GRAY and WHITE
Colors all around!

(Verse 2)   RED on stop lights
YELLOW sunshine
BLUE for sky and sea
GREEN for grass and
ORANGE for oranges
PURPLE grapes for me!

(Verse 3)   BROWN for rich earth
BLACK for tires
PINK for ribbons tied,
GRAY for elephant
WHITE for snow, we're learning
Colors on the Jolly Trolley Ride!
(Repeat Verse 1)

Circle Song

We're Marching, We're Marching
We're Marching around the **CIRCLES**
We're Marching, We're Marching
We're Marching around the **CIRCLES**
Round and round, round and round
We're Marching around the **CIRCLES**
Learning about the shapes as we go!
(Sing each verse 3 times)

Rectangle Song

We're Marching, We're Marching
We're Marching around the **RECTANGLES**
We're Marching, We're Marching
We're Marching around the **RECTANGLES**
Two long sides, two short sides
We're Marching around the **RECTANGLES**
Learning about the shapes as we go!
(Sing each verse 3 times)

Square Song

We're Marching, We're Marching
We're Marching around the **SQUARES** just so
We're Marching, We're Marching
We're Marching around the **SQUARES** just so
Four corners, four sides
We're Marching around the **SQUARES** just so
Learning about the shapes as we go!
(Sing each verse 3 times)

Triangle Song

We're Marching, we're Marching
We're Marching around the **TRIANGLES**
We're Marching, we're Marching
We're Marching around the **TRIANGLES**
Three corners, three sides
We're Marching around the **TRIANGLES**
Learning about the shapes as we go!
(Sing each verse 3 times)

Shape Review Song

We're Marching, we're Marching
We're Marching around the **TRIANGLES**
We're Marching, we're Marching
We're Marching around the **TRIANGLES**
Three corners, three sides
We're Marching around the **TRIANGLES**
Learning about the shapes as we go!

We're Marching, We're Marching
We're Marching around the **SQUARES** just so
We're Marching, We're Marching
We're Marching around the **SQUARES** just so
Four corners, four sides
We're Marching around the **SQUARES** just so
Learning about the shapes as we go!

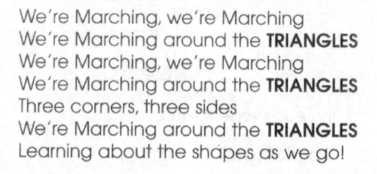

We're Marching, We're Marching
We're Marching around the **CIRCLES**
We're Marching, We're Marching
We're Marching around the **CIRCLES**
Round and round, round and round
We're Marching around the **CIRCLES**
Learning about the shapes as we go!

We're Marching, We're Marching
We're Marching around the **RECTANGLES**
We're Marching, We're Marching
We're Marching around the **RECTANGLES**
Two long sides, two short sides
We're Marching around the **RECTANGLES**
Learning about the shapes as we go!

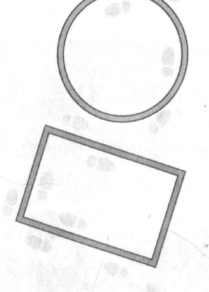

Music
Preschool Readiness Activities

Looby Loo

(Verse 1)
(Do actions)

I put my **RIGHT HAND** in
I put my **RIGHT HAND** out
I give my **RIGHT HAND** a shake, shake, shake
and turn myself about.

CHORUS
(Circle Left)

Here we go Looby Loo
Here we go Looby Lie
Here we go Looby Loo
On a Saturday night

Verse 2

I put my **LEFT HAND** in
I put my **LEFT HAND** out
I give my **LEFT HAND** a shake, shake, shake
And turn myself about.
　　(Go to chorus)

Verse 3

I put my **RIGHT FOOT** in
I put my **RIGHT FOOT** out
I give my **RIGHT FOOT** a shake, shake, shake
and turn myself about.
　　(Go to chorus)

Verse 4

I put my **LEFT FOOT** in
I put my **LEFT FOOT** out
I give my **LEFT FOOT** a shake, shake, shake
and turn myself about.
　　(Go to chorus)

Verse 5

I put my **WHOLE SELF** in
I put my **WHOLE SELF** out
I give my **WHOLE SELF** a shake, shake, shake
and turn myself about.
　　(Go to chorus)

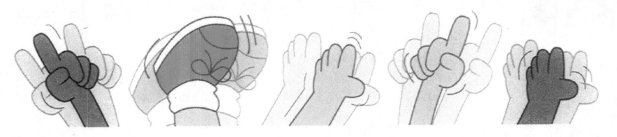

Music
Preschool Readiness Activities

Alphabet Lane Song

A	says	ă,	do you hear it in	apple?
B	says	bh,	do you hear it in	ball?
C	says	ck,	do you hear it in	cat?
D	says	dh,	do you hear it in	doll?
E	says	ĕh,	do you hear it in	egg?
F	says	ff,	do you hear it in	fan?
G	says	gh,	do you hear it in	goat?
H	says	h,	do you hear it in	hand?
I	says	ĭ,	do you hear it in	inchworm?
J	says	j,	do you hear it in	jam?
K	says	ck,	do you hear it in	kite?
L	says	ll,	do you hear it in	lamb?
M	says	m,	do you hear it in	monkey?
N	says	n,	do you hear it in	noodles?
O	says	ŏ,	do you hear it in	octopus?
P	says	p,	do you hear it in	poodles?
Q	says	kw,	do you hear it in	quilt?
R	says	r,	do you hear it in	rail?
S	says	ss,	do you hear it in	sun?
T	says	t,	do you hear it in	tail?
U	says	ŭ,	do you hear it in	umbrella?
V	says	v,	do you hear it in	vase?
W	says	w,	do you hear it in	wagon?

Look at me, See a happy face!

X	says	x(ks),	do you hear it in	fox?
Y	says	y,	do you hear it in	yarn?
Z	says	z,	do you hear it in	zoo?

We've come a long way and we're at the big barn!

On Alphabet Lane we're learning our letters
And all their sounds from A to Z.
When we learn them well we'll be ready to read,
Just come along with us and you will see.

A to Z Phonics Song

When we learn these sounds, you'll see, ready to read then, we will be.

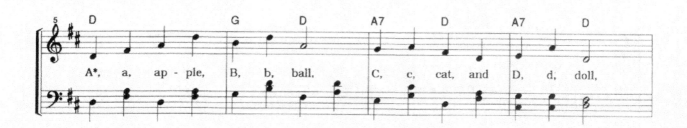

A*, a, ap-ple, B, b, ball, C, c, cat, and D, d, doll,

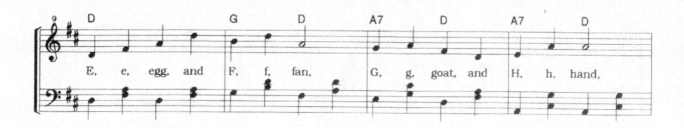

E, e, egg, and F, f, fan, G, g, goat, and H, h, hand,

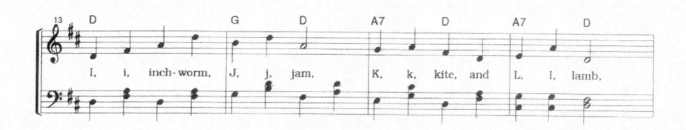

I, i, inch-worm, J, j, jam, K, k, kite, and L, l, lamb,

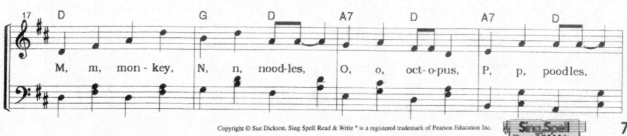

M, m, mon-key, N, n, nood-les, O, o, oct-o-pus, P, p, poodles,

Music
Preschool Readiness Activities

A-Z Phonics Song (continued)

Q, q, quilt, and R, r, rail, S, s, sun, and T, t, tail,

U, u, um-brel-la, V, v, vase, I'm nearly through, see my hap-py face

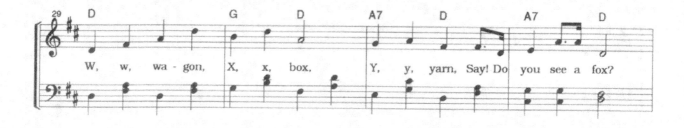

W, w, wa-gon, X, x, box, Y, y, yarn, Say! Do you see a fox?

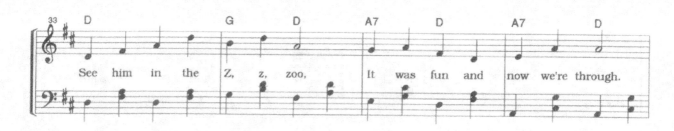

See him in the Z, z, zoo, It was fun and now we're through.

Da Capo

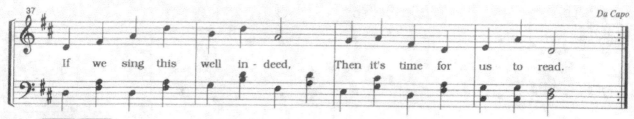

If we sing this well in-deed, Then it's time for us to read.